Comets

Experts on child reading levels
have consulted on the level of text and
concepts in this book.

At the end of the book is a "Look Back and Find" section
which provides additional information and encourages
the child to refer back to previous pages
for the answers to the questions posed.

Angela Grunsell trained as a teacher in 1969.
She has a Diploma in Reading and Related Skills
and for the last five years has advised London
teachers on materials and resources.

Published in the United States in 1985 by
Franklin Watts, 387 Park Avenue South, New York, NY 10016

© Aladdin Books Ltd/Franklin Watts

Designed and produced by
Aladdin Books Ltd, 70 Old Compton Street, London W1

ISBN 0 531 10024 3

Library of Congress Number:
85-50511

Printed in Italy
by Arti Grafiche Vincenzo Bona - Torino

FRANKLIN · WATTS · FIRST · LIBRARY

Comets

by
Kate Petty

Consultant
Angela Grunsell

Illustrated by
Mike Saunders

Franklin Watts
New York · London · Toronto · Sydney

Have you ever seen a comet in the sky?
It looks like a beautiful, bright star
with a long tail.

Comets don't appear very often. When a comet does appear it can be seen night after night, sometimes for weeks. It seems to hang in the sky, its tail streaming out into space.

How big is a comet? The ball of rock and ice
that forms the center of a large comet
is several miles across.

The bright cloud of gas around the middle
is called the coma.
The tail is made from gas and dust.
It can stretch for millions of miles.

There are millions of comets in a great cloud at the outermost edges of the Solar System. The comets we see have gone into orbit around the Sun.

The shape of a comet's orbit is like a long oval.
At one end of its journey it loops around the Sun.
At the other end it is far out in space.

A comet can only be seen when it comes close
to the Sun and is lit up by it. The bright
coma and streaming tail are formed as some of
the ices turn to gas in the heat of the Sun.

The picture shows a comet at different stages
of its journey as it passes close to the Sun.
The tail always points away from the Sun.

A comet's tail is formed from dust particles as well as gas. Sometimes the dust and gas separate into two or more tails.

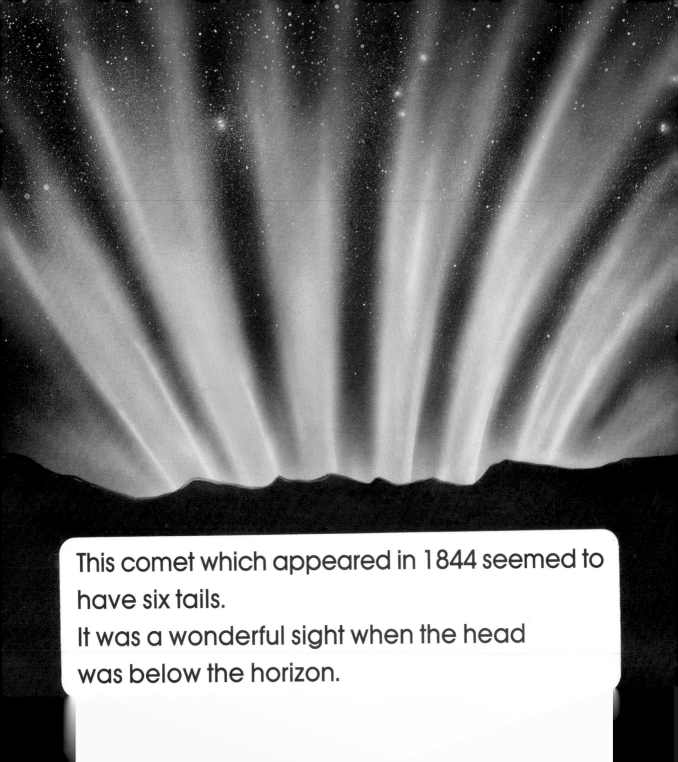

This comet which appeared in 1844 seemed to have six tails.
It was a wonderful sight when the head was below the horizon.

A scientist named Edmond Halley calculated that
one special comet was seen every 76 years.
Can you see it in this tapestry of 1066,
which shows the death of King Harold of England?

16

People used to think comets were bad omens.
When Halley's Comet appeared in 1835
it looked like a sword hanging in the sky.

Halley's Comet last appeared in 1910.
These observers hoped to get a closer view
of it from the basket of a balloon.

In the nineteenth century there were many other bright comets. The Great Comet of 1843 had a tail as long as the distance between Earth and Mars.

A comet disappears from our sight leaving
a trail of dust in its path. When Earth passes
through a trail, specks of the dust
fall through our atmosphere and burn up.

These burning streaks are called meteors
or "shooting stars." On a cloudless night
you might spot one or two. In November 1833
these meteors showered down like snowflakes.

Larger meteors are more likely to be pieces of rock from the asteroid belt. Those which fall to Earth are called meteorites. This meteorite in South Africa weighs more than 60 tons.

The crater in the Arizona Desert is more than half a mile wide. It was made when a meteorite hit the Earth 22,000 years ago.
Pieces of the meteorite have been found near by.

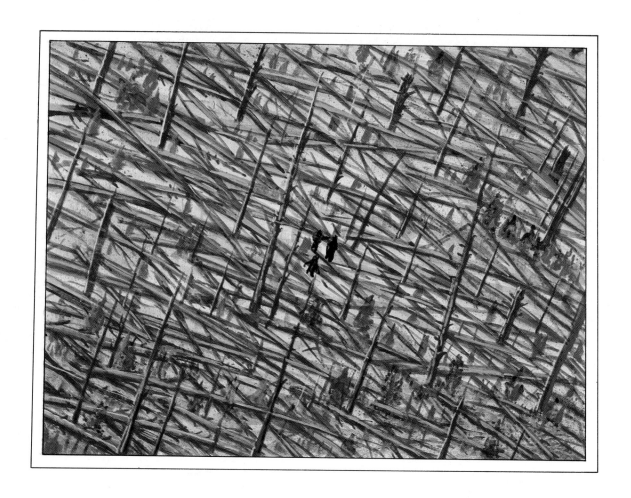

In 1908 a bright object fell from the sky and destroyed a forest in Siberia. No traces of the object were ever found, so it might have been an icy comet that simply melted away.

This comet crashed into the Sun. The first
picture shows it heading toward the Sun.
The second picture shows the dust storm
around the Sun after the comet broke up.

Halley's Comet revisits Earth in 1986. Astronomers can study it more closely than ever before. Spacecraft *Giotto's* flight takes it close to the center of the comet.

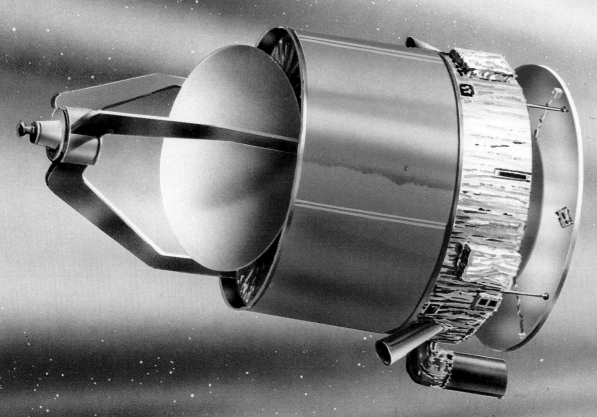

Giotto and other spacecraft are sending back pictures telling us more about comets and space beyond the Solar System.

Halley's Comet will not return until 2062.

Look back and find

What is the nucleus of the comet?
*It is the ball of rock and ices
in the middle of the comet.*

How big is a comet compared with a planet?
*A planet is a huge world; a comet is
more like a large field; so a comet is tiny
compared with a planet.*

Where did comets come from in the
first place?
*Comets are probably made from dust and
gas left over when the Solar System
was formed more than 4 billion years ago.*

How is a comet's orbit different from a
planet's orbit?

Does a comet have any light of its own?

When does a comet become visible to us?

What happens to a comet as it passes
close to the Sun?

When did the astronomer Edmond Halley live?
About 300 years ago, from 1656 to 1742.

Why do you think the people who made this tapestry long ago chose to show the comet?
They thought the appearance of the comet was connected with all the bad things that had happened.

When does a meteor shower like this happen?
When the Earth passes through the thickest part of the trail left by a comet.

What would happen if the Earth passed through the actual tail of a comet?
Earth passed through the tail of Halley's Comet in 1910 with no ill effects.

What spacecraft other than *Giotto* will be finding out about Halley's Comet?
The Russians are sending two Vega probes. The Japanese probe is called Planet A.

Why has no one sent a spacecraft to find out about Halley's Comet before?

Index